Preceding pages 1: A Tibetan boy is all curiosity as he gazes at the world through window panes: Tingri, Western Tibet.
Pages 2-3: Kunlun mountains of Northern Tibet (Changthang), the land of nomads, rich in wild life.
Pages 4-5: Gurla Mandata mountain ranges.
Pages 6-7: Ganden Monastery, one of the largest monasteries near Lhasa, was badly damaged during the 1960s Cultural Revolution.

Decorated doorway of Tulok monastery in Northern Tibet.

Following pages: (title page) Lhasa grandmother spinning her prayer wheel with her loyal dog beside her.
Pages 10-11: Mt. Everest, East Face, called Chomolhari by Tibetans, considered sacred for both Tibetans and Nepalese.
Pages 12-13: A typical scene in front of Jokhang Temple (Lhasa), which is considered the most holy temple in Tibet.
Pages 14-15: Distant view of Potala, the palace of the Dalai Lamas since the 17th century.
Page 18: Each monastic town or village has its own local festivals and ceremonies. This picture shows the summer festival in Changra, Derge (Kham) in which local lamas participate.

TIBET

Yeshi Choedon
Dawa Norbu

Lustre Press
Roli Books

CHINA

Historical Map of Tibet

KUN LUN RANGE

GOLMUD

A

RUTOG

C H A N G   T H A N G
DESERT

NGARI

THOLING

TANGLA RANGE

TSAPARANG

RETING

Mt. KAILASH

MANASAROVAR

U   T   S   A   N   G

PURANG

KONGP

TACHILUNPO

NEPAL

LHAZE   SHIGATSE   LHASA

SAKYA   TSANGPO RIVER

KATHMANDU GAURI SHANKAR Mt.   TINGRI   GYANTSE   K

TSETHANG

Mt. EVEREST

BHUTAN

----- KATHMANDU-LHASA HIGHWAY

BRAHMAPUTRA RIVER

INDIA

BANGLA
DESH   INDIA

DO

DERGE

CHAMDO

DRAYAB

KHAM

BURMA

CONTENTS

17

PRELUDE

When our publishers suggested that we write a text for a picture book on Tibet, we were a bit hesitant. For there are already so many pictorial works and coffee table books on Tibet. On second thought, however, we felt that there is a need for a concise and comprehensive book which can convey the spirit of Tibetan culture and history through both photographs and words.

While envisaging such a book in our minds, we have tried our level best to do justice to the mysterious complexity of Tibetan history and culture within the limitations of space. We have tried to convey the spirit of Tibetan history through myths as well as historical facts, as these are found inextricably interwoven in Tibetan historical texts. We have also tried to give a fair and balanced coverage to all the periods of Tibetan history, even though we might have privileged, as we realised later, the Dalai Lama period more than others. We hope this is justified.

Tibetan religion is not a monolith, as it might appear to the general public. Tibetan Buddhism consists of four major sects, each characterised by a particular guru-lineage system originating in ancient India, distinct philosophical interpretations of Madhyamika philosophy, specific sectarian ritual practices, and different monastic organisations. Such specificities have, over the centuries, contributed to the rich diversity and the philosophical depth of Tibetan religious culture and civilisation. This also reflects Buddhist Tibet's fairly successful practice of cultural pluralism. We have made a sincere effort to give a balanced and fair coverage to each of the sects, describing their essential characteristics. We have also discussed Bon, the pre-Buddhist native religion of Tibet.

We hope we have given a glimpse of Tibetan literature, which is absolutely vast, in our sections on religion and history. The only omission might be art. Finally, we have abstained from political subjects in this text, which is essentially on religion, culture and social history.

While preparing this text, we have benefited from the resources of Jawaharlal Nehru University Library and Tibet House Library, New Delhi. We are grateful to the Tibet House director, Lama Doboom Tulku, and his staff and to Jawaharlal Nehru University Acting Librarian, Sri B.N. Rao and staff for all their help. Finally, we would like to thank our publishers, Mr Pramod Kapoor and Ms Bela Butalia, for their keen interest in this project.

Yeshi Choedon
Dawa Norbu

THE LAND
OF SNOWS...

AND ITS
PEOPLE

Tibet has fascinated the imagination of humankind for a long time. It has been known to the world as a forbidden and mystical land. To the natural difficulties of entering Tibet and of travelling in its bleak uplands had been added the spirit of seclusion which had moved its government to keep foreigners out of their sacred Buddhist land. Standing thus alone in the midst of snow mountains, Tibet differs greatly from its neighbours. She differs not only in her physical features, in her flora and fauna, but also in her government and her people, in language, folklore, religious traditions and culture.

Land

Tibet stretches 2,000 kilometres from India in the west to China in the east, and a 1,000 kilometres from Nepal in the south to the Chinese province of Xinjiang (Turkistan) in the north. Its average elevation is 4,000 metres above sea level. On three sides it is bordered by some of the loftiest mountains in the world; to the south by the mighty Himalaya, to the west by the Karakoram ranges and to the north by the Kunlun and Thangla ranges. From somewhere near the northern-most point of the frontier, the land gradually descends eastwards, its vast barren spaces interrupted by subsidiary mountain ranges and deep gorges, until it meets the lowlands of China's western-most provinces of Sichuan and Yunnan.

Some of Asia's greatest rivers have their sources on the Tibetan plateau. Tsangpo, the great river, rises near Mount Kailash (Tesi in Tibetan) and Lake Manasarovar (Mapham Tso in Tibetan) in the west of Tibet. After flowing to the east, it leaves Tibet with a great sweep southwards into Assam, where its name changes to Brahmaputra.

The source of the Tsangpo lies quite close to those of two other major rivers, the Indus and the Sutlej, flowing in the opposite direction from east to west and then turning south. In the far east of the country, the Machu (Huangho) and the Drichu (Yangtse) rivers flow due east, while the Gyalmo Ngulchu (Salween) and the Zachu (Mekong) rivers begin their long journey in Southeast Asia.

Tibet can be divided by nature and climatic features into three main regions: (a) The Northern Plain, (b) Southern Tibet, and (c) Eastern Tibet.

The northern half of Tibet is a virtually uninhabited desert called Changthang (northern plain). Only occasional hunters and collectors of salt and borax roam this barren wasteland. It is situated at altitudes of above 4,500 metres and the general altitude declines from northwest to southeast. Because of the extreme climate and altitude, there are virtually no forests in this region. The south of this plain is famous for its extensive pastures and grasslands. These pastures are inhabited by a spare, scattered population of nomads and possess a relatively high percentage of domestic animals like sheep, goats and yaks. Wild animals such as wild yaks (drong), wild asses (kyang), wild sheep, wild goats, antelopes, wolves and other animals are traditionally numerous in the Changthang. The nomads of this region live in tents, surviving on meat and dairy products. Periodically, they bring supplies of dried meat, wool, butter and cheese from the highlands into the towns and trade them for *tsampa* (barley flour), cloth and simple manufactured goods. In terms of area, this is the largest of Tibet's regions. comprising over 45 per cent of its total extent.

Southern Tibet comprises mainly trans-Himalayan mountains and the valley of the Tsangpo (Brahmaputra) as well as its various tributaries. Altitudes vary from well above 6,000 metres in the western part of the region, and along the Himalayan ranges, Tesi and Thangla mountains, to above 1,000 metres in the east, where the Tsangpo enters India. The majority of Tibetans live in this area irrigated by the Tsangpo river and its tributaries. These more hospitable regions of generally protected valleys produce the crops upon which the Tibetans depend: barley, wheat and a small variety of

Preceding pages 20-21: Yaks in the Himalaya, below Gauri Shankar Peak, Kathmandu-Lhasa highway.
Pages 22-23: Village men gather together at Kathok Monastery (a famous Nyingmapa monastery in Kham).

Prayer flags at North Face of sacred Mt. Kailash, which is considered
holy both by Hindus and Buddhists.

vegetables. Animal husbandry is also practised and on the farms you will find cows, goats, pigs and horses. There are numerous scattered villages.

Some of the great towns of Tibet, like Shigatse, Gyantse, Lhasa, are found in this region. Lhasa has been the capital of Tibet since ancient times. Other towns are the centres of trade and the seats of governors. Above all, the two most important provinces of Tibet, U and Tsang, which together from U-Tsang are found in this region. In fact, southern Tibet is the cradle of Tibetan culture and civilisation.

Eastern Tibet consists of the steep valleys and mountains located between Gangkar Chogley Namgyal, Minyak Gangkar and Khawakarpo ranges. In south-eastern Tibet we find Drichu (Yangtse), Zachu (Mekong) and Gyalmo Nyulchu (Salween), three of the largest rivers in Asia, flowing in deep, parallel gorges close to each other. Dense evergreen forests are

an outstanding feature of the region, covering 18 per cent of the land area, while another 42 per cent is grassland. On the whole, this area lies at more reasonable elevations. Among all of Tibet's regions, the eastern region possesses the natural factors conducive to intensive agriculture. As a whole, it comprises about 30 per cent of Tibet's total area.

People

The origin of the Tibetans is still a mystery. Theories put forward about it are based on all sorts of observations—ethnographic, linguistic, and the like—and postulate various migrations of different peoples. Tibetans have several ethnogenic myths but the most popular one since the Buddhist revolution is as follows: the Tibetan people, as a race, trace their parentage to a forest monkey, specifically from a male monkey, an incarnation of the deity

Tibet used to be rich in wild life. A herd of kyang (wild asses) seen galloping across the vastness of the Tibetan plateau.

the population of Tibetans are divergent in nature. A survey of Western sources shows that it is impossible to pin-point the number of Tibetans with any accuracy. Lack of a detailed census and of general statistics contribute to a situation where some guesswork will have to take the place of hard facts. William Rockhill, at the turn of the century, gave the figure of 3.5 million for all Tibetans (in his book, *The Land of Lamas)*, out of whom about 2 million were supposed to inhabit the "kingdom of Lhasa." David Macdonald, a British trade agent in Tibet, estimates the population to be 3.9 million. The estimates made by the Dalai Lama place the total population of the three Tibetan

Preceding pages 30-31: Summer horse-racing, which used to be a popular sport among nomads and peasants in Tibet. This picture shows horse owners camping for the festival in Paiyual, Kham (Eastern Tibet).

provinces of U-Tsang, Kham and Amdo at 6 million. On the other hand, the Chinese authority gives the figure of just 2.77 million Tibetan population. Like the Chinese authority, some Western scholars seem to consider Tibet as comprising the U-Tsang region alone, a practice that results in substantial under-estimations of population.

Civilisation

Although Buddhism has had a strong influence on the evolution of Tibetan culture, Tibet's civilisation predates Buddhism and was shaped initially by the Bon religion. Tibetan people have not only a common culture, they possess a unique civilisation that is comparable to other great civilisations of Europe and the East. Since the mid-twentieth century, Tibetan religious and cultural centres have been established all over

Camel caravan along the Kunlun Mountains of Northern Tibet (Changthang).

the world due to the keen interest shown by various people, especially Westerners.

The earlier generation of Western linguists classified the Tibetan language as belonging to the Tibeto-Burmese family of languages. Since the mid-1950s it has been broadly reclassified as falling within a broader linguistic family called Sino-Tibetan. Both are based on the assumptions of hypothetical ancestor languages (Proto-Tibet-Burma and Proto-Sino-Tibetan) which are no longer in existence. Tibetan has had a writing system since the seventh century. The script is borrowed from an Indian prototype but Tibetan itself is unrelated to Sanskrit or any other Indic language. It has a vast literature and is considered by many to be among the Asian languages second only to Chinese in the depth of its historical record.

There are some regional dialects within the spoken language such as Lhasa, Golok, Tsang, Kham, and so on, but it is unified by a single writing system propagated by lama missionaries and the Lhasa administration. Further, regional dialects are inter-communicable. The peculiarity of dialects is due to their different accents (phonology). Thus the Tibetan people enjoy a high degree of linguistic unity which they call *bod-kad* and absolute uniformity in writing with two basic scripts of *uchen* and *umed*.

The Tibetan people follow a common religion which was previously called lamaism and now appreciatively known as Tibetan Buddhism. However, it would be fair to state that Tibetan religion is not a monolith. Being one of the most complex religious systems in the world, it has four major sects, that is, the Nyingmapa, Kagyupa, Sakyapa and Gelugpa. These sects have added a rich diversity in terms of different guru lineages, philosophical interpretations and ritual

Prayer-flags on top of a La (high pass) on the Lhasa-Kathmandu highway. Tibetans believe (as per the pre-Buddhist Bon belief), that spirits and deities reside on high places like mountains, hilltops or passes.

practices. However, these diversities developed within a basic unity. The basic unity stems from the fact that all the sects accept the two Tibetan Buddhist canons, the *Kagyur* and the *Tangyur*, as their foundational texts. Further, the sects are not concentrated in particular areas or regions, except Lhasa and Sakya, which would have been a destabilising factor in Tibetan society. They are spread throughout the Tibetan plateau in close proximity to each other, thereby encouraging cultural interaction and healthy competition. Sectarian affiliations did not apply to the lay people who broadly described themselves as

non-pa—'those who are in the fold of Buddhist law(s)'—and generally respected all the Buddhist sects.

The formation of sects within Tibetan Buddhism represented the Tibetanisation of Buddhism to such a degree that it has become uniquely Tibetan. The process, however, did not distort the essence and logic of the Buddha-Nagarjuna philosophy. It refined and elaborated Buddhist philosophy and practice to such a high degree that it has become world famous. However, apart from Buddhists, who form the overwhelming majority, there are Bonpos, Christians and Muslims in Tibet.

Facing page: Khampa nomads with their modern rifles in Kham, East Tibet.

MYSTERY...

AND
HISTORY

The early history of Tibet is obscure. The number of historical works written by Tibetans is not small but they deal chiefly with religious happenings and abound in myths and miracles. Historically Tibet was ruled by royal lineages for almost a thousand years from around 127 BC. The royal lineage began with Nyatri Tsenpo, who was believed to have made a magical descent from the skies. This man appeared on a mountain called Yarlha Zhampo which is found at the head of the Yarlung valley in Central Tibet. When the people of the region asked where he came from, the man, not understanding their language, gestured skyward and they, thinking he must be very holy to have come from the sky, decided to make him their leader. Placing him on a wooden sedan-chair, they carried him on their shoulders to their home and there gave him the name Nyatri Tsenpo, meaning "Neck-enthroned King." They built a palace known as Yumbulagang, which is still to be seen in Central Tibet. Nyatri Tsenpo and the next six kings are said to have returned to the sky after death by means of a "sky-rope," and hence no tombs for them are known.

The tomb of the eighth king is said to exist in Kongpo in the U-Tsang region. The eighth king's name was Drigum Tsenpo and it is from his time that the real history of Tibet begins. Since Drigum Tsenpo was buried in a tomb, it is assumed that he accidentally cut the "sky-rope" and could not ascend to heaven at death, as his ancestors had done.

The first twenty-seven kings of the Yarlung dynasty adhered to the native Bon religion. Bon was an animistic cult governed by exorcists, shamans and priests, the early nature of which remains veiled behind centuries of Buddhist antagonism and Bon's own self-imposed transformation as a means of keeping up with the Buddhists. During the reign of the twenty-eighth king, Lha tho-tho-ri Nyantsen, the first Buddhist scriptures appeared in Tibet. They were believed to have descended from the sky. Nobody could read the book of scriptures because it was in Sanskrit. The king named the book *Nyenpo Sangwa* (The Secret), and told his ministers that he had been shown in a dream that after four generations there would be a king able to read and understand the sacred book.

Four generations later, Namri Songtsen, the thirty-second king, had a son named Songtsen Gampo. Songtsen Gampo, who ascended the throne at the age of thirteen in AD 630, adopted an expansionist policy and carried on his war-like activities towards neighbouring countries. Tibetan forces were active at the time from the plains of northern India to the Chinese frontiers in the east, and the borders of the Turkish empire in the west. Under Gampo's leadership Tibet emerged as a formidable **military power in Central Asia and established a** powerful empire. He moved the capital from Yarlung to Lhasa and built a palace on the Red Hill (the site of the Potala Palace).

Perhaps one of the highlights of the Tibetan campaigns was Songtsen Gampo's 2,000,000 strong army marching into China and demanding Princess Wenchen Gungchu in marriage from the Tang Emperor. The Chinese fought a battle but were defeated and so the emperor finally agreed to give the princess in marriage. The princess was referred to by the Tibetans as *"Gyasa,"* which means "The Chinese Consort." She arrived at Lhasa with articles of personal use such as silk, porcelain, and an image of Sakyamuni, the Gautama Buddha. As this image is also said to have been blessed by the Lord Buddha himself, the Tibetans considered it to be very sacred.

Earlier, the king had sent his minister, Gar Tongtsen, with presents and a letter to the Nepalese King Amshuvarman, to ask for the hand of Princess Bhrikuti Devi in marriage. Amshuvarman sent his daughter to Songtsen Gampo and she took with her an image of the Buddha. That image is considered sacred by the Tibetans as it is also said to have been blessed

Preceding pages 36-37: The stark beauty of this rugged Tibetan landscape provides the right setting for monastic life.
Pages 38-39: Temples and monasteries of Lhasa in a typical Tibetan-style painting. Potala Palace is shown surrounded by Drepung, Sera and Ganden monasteries.

by Lord Buddha himself. The Tibetans always refer to the Princess Bhrikuti Devi as *"Belsa,"* which means "The Nepalese Consort."

Both Gyasa and Belsa wished to build temples for the images of the Buddha they had brought to Tibet. Gyasa had her temple built and called it Ramoche Tsukla-khang. Belsa, lacking the necessary astrological guidance, asked Gyasa for advice on the location for her temple and Gyasa advised her to build it over a small lake. Wondering if Gyasa was misleading her out of jealousy, Belsa spoke to Songtsen Gampo, who confirmed, after prayer and meditation, that the correct site was over a small lake. The Tibetans built her temple by filling in the small lake with logs and earth, which had been carried there by a large number of goats. After the temple was completed, an image of a goat was erected beside it in honour of those animals. The temple was called Rasa Trulnang Tsukla-Khang, and later became known as the Jokhang. The door of Gyasa's temple faced east towards China and that of Belsa's faced west towards Nepal. During the next generation, the two images were interchanged in the temples for reasons of security when it was rumoured that a Chinese army was about to enter Lhasa.

Religious Consolidation

In course of time, Songtsen Gampo became aware of the Buddhist culture prevailing not only in India but also as an inspiring force in the newly formed Tang dynasty of China. The prestige and significance of Buddhism was further impressed upon him by his Nepalese and Chinese wives. Therefore he played a pioneering role in establishing Buddhism in Tibet. In order that the sacred religious books be translated, a written script needed to be invented. Songtsen Gampo sent his minister, Thon-mi Sam-bhota, with sixteen companions to India to learn the language. Thon-mi Sam-bhota went to Kashmir in northwest India, where he had as his tutors the well known Buddhist masters, Lipi Kara and Devavidyasimha. The Tibetan students who accompanied him to India died there. After Thon-mi Sam-bhota returned to Tibet he used his knowledge of the Brahmi and

Gupta scripts to devise a Tibetan script. He then is said to have translated the book, *The Secret*, preserved since the time of Lha tho-tho-ri Nyantsen, and so its enlightening contents were made known to the people. During Songtsen Gampo's reign many Buddhist scriptures were translated into the Tibetan language. He also built many temples throughout the land. His Chinese queen Gyasa had discovered through astrology that Tibet was "like a female demon lying on its back." So the religious shrines were built in those parts of Tibet which corresponded with the arms and hands, and the legs and feet of the demon, thereby lessening its power. There was considerable opposition to the construction of shrines but the work carried on. Songtsen Gampo also introduced a legal code for the nation based on the teachings of the Buddha. He established laws for the punishment of murder, robbery and adultery. He encouraged learning and practice of the sixteen righteous duties. In short, he gave a strong religious impulse to the whole of Tibet.

The Tibetan queen of Songtsen Gampo, Mongsa Tricham of Tolung, gave birth to a son named Gungsong Gungtsen. At the age of thirteen he ascended the throne. He ruled for only five years and died at the age of eighteen. Songtsen Gampo has left an indelible imprint in ruling over Tibet. As a conqueror, a legislator and a religious and educational reformer, Songsten Gampo has left an indelible imprint in Tibetan annals. Among the Tibetan kings, Songtsen Gampo is invariably referred to as Choegyal. Choegyal is the Tibetan translation of the Sanskrit term "Dharmaraja," meaning a ruler who rules not only in accordance with the holy doctrine, but also one who patronises *dharma* (that which is established by law, duty or custom but implying Buddhism or *buddhadharma* here).

Songtsen Gampo died in AD 649: his tomb is located in the Chongya valley near Yarlung. He was succeeded to the throne by his grandson, Mangsong Mangtsen, who was only a

Following pages 42-43: Of the many offerings to deities, butter-lamp offering is the most popular one in monasteries and private chapels: a butter-lamp offering at Jokhang, Lhasa.

child at the time. Therefore, Gar Tongtsen, the trusted minister of Songtsen Gampo, acted as regent until the boy came of age. The imperial tasks and pious deeds initiated by Songtsen Gampo were carried on by the successive kings who competed fiercely with other nations for domination of Central Asia.

The second great ruler of the Yarlung dynasty, Trisong Detsen, did not begin his reign until 755, more than a hundred years after the death of Songtsen Gampo. He inherited a strong empire, consolidated by the four kings who had ruled since Songtsen Gampo, and launched further military expeditions into China and India. Buddhism had not progressed much and the country was still very much in the grip of the Bon tradition. In the face of considerable resistance from Bon factions in the court, Trisong Detsen started a wide-scale restoration of Buddhist temples erected by Songtsen Gampo and invited a number of notable Indian Buddhist masters to Tibet.

Trisong Detsen wanted to encourage the spread of Buddhism but he found himself opposed by many of his ministers, who were devoted to the Bon religion. Mashang Dompa Ke and Takra Lugong were two ministers strongly opposed to the Buddhist faith. There were also two junior ministers, Gos Trizang and Shang Nyamzang, who were willing to help the king patronise the Buddhist religion, and who approached various sympathetic ministers, apprising the latter of their intention to raise a certain issue in the council and asking them for their support. Then they bribed an oracle to predict a great famine and epidemic for the country and a short life for the king unless two loyal subjects offered themselves as sacrifices for the welfare of the king and the country.

The traditional account is that Gos, the pro-Buddhist minister, and Mashang, the pro-Bon minister, were the two who were to be entombed in accordance with the prophecy. Gos, who had instigated the scheme, had made secret arrangements and escaped from the tomb, leaving Mashang to die. There is another account, which says that the prophecy was that two prominent people had to go into exile as ransom. An assembly of ministers was called to discuss the issue and the two junior ministers, Gos and Shang, stood up and declared their long-standing loyalty to the king and volunteered to go into exile. This gesture was received warmly by the assembly and the two ministers were praised for their spirit of self-sacrifice.

The two senior ministers, Mashang Dompa Ke and Takra Lugong, seeing that this could result in loss of face for them, protested and insisted that not only were they the senior ministers, but they were of greater loyalty than anyone else. Therefore, they should be given the honour of going into exile. The assembly approved their request.

There are other accounts also. Whatever these might be, it is clear that once Mashang was removed from the scene, King Trisong Detsen sent one of his ministers, Ba Salnang, to Nepal to invite the Indian *pandit*, Santiraksita, to come to Tibet and teach Buddhism. Santiraksita accepted the invitation, and when he arrived at Drakmar he was warmly welcomed by the Tibetan king. After he began to preach, the Bon spirits of the country were so resentful and displeased that they caused storms, lightning, and floods to take place. The people interpreted these omens as a sign that the new religion was not acceptable and Santiraksita, sensing that the time was not yet ripe for the spread of his teachings, returned to Nepal. Before departing, however, he suggested to the king that he should invite the great Indian Tantric master, Padmasambhava, to visit Tibet.

Ba Salnang was sent again to invite Padmasambhava, who was in Nepal at the time. Padmasambhava was well versed in the Tantric form of Buddhism, which was more acceptable to the Tibetan people. Tibetan tradition makes Padmasambhava out to be a native of the land of Uddiyana, which was famous for its magicians. It also links him with the land of Zahor where Tantrism flourished, a country sometimes described as being in northwest India, sometimes in Bengal. He was welcomed by the king himself. Padmasambhava was able to subdue the Bon spirits, who had opposed his missionary efforts in Tibet. He subdued them and made them take an oath to defend

Phurburchog Temple: a hilltop temple of Rig-sum-gonpo, the three protecting
Bodhisattvas of Tibet and therefore popular deities among Tibetan Buddhists.

the new religion. Thus many of these spirits
were taken into the Buddhist pantheon.
Padmasambhava became one of the patron
saints of Tibet, and the chief saint of the Red
Hat sect, the followers of the original Buddhism
of Tibet. Among the Red Hat sect, his image
occupies the place of honour on Tibetan altars
as often as that of Buddha himself.

Santiraksita was again invited back to
Tibet. The king decided to have a monastery
built and Santiraksita drew up the plans,
using as his model the monastery of
Odantapuri, which was laid out in the design
of the Buddhist universe. The monastery was
built in Drakmar, which is fifty miles
southeast of Lhasa. When it was completed
after twelve years, it was called Migyur
Lhungi Dubpai Tsukla-khang, meaning "The
Temple which is an Unchangeable, Perfect
Mass." It is commonly referred to as Samye

Monastery. It is the oldest of the large
monasteries in Tibet.

Around 779, the king selected seven
intelligent men to be ordained as monks by
Santiraksita. They were trained by Santiraksita
and they became the first monks in Tibet. A
school for the study of Sanskrit was established
at Samye and a large number of Buddhist texts
from India were translated into the Tibetan
language. But the prominent role played by
Indian teachers at the time must not lead us to
overlook the equally strong influence of Chinese
Buddhism.

At the request of the Tibetan king, China
sent two Buddhist monks in 781, who were
skilled in preaching. They were to be replaced
by others every two years, as a permanent
arrangement. Probably in 791, the king issued
an edict establishing Buddhism as the official
religion. The text of the edict was carved on a

pillar near Samye. In course of time, there arose a conflict between the two schools of Buddhism prevailing in Tibet. The first school taught that enlightenment was an instantaneous realisation that could be attained only through complete mental and physical inactivity, and this was being propagated by the Chinese monks. The other school maintained that enlightenment was the result of a slow, gradual process, requiring study, analysis and good deeds, and this teaching was being propagated by the Indian teachers.

Faced with the ensuing outburst of doctrinal antagonism between adherents of Indian and Chinese Buddhism, the king decided to hold a religious debate, the kind of rhetorical and theological duel that was then in vogue in India and China. Hoshang, a Chinese monk, defended the "instantaneous system" and Kamalasila, an Indian disciple of Santiraksita, defended the "slow system." The debate seems to have taken place at Samye over a two-year period (792-794) in the king's presence. The Chinese lost and were forced to leave the country. The king proclaimed that only the doctrine that had been maintained by the Indian Buddhist masters was to be recognised in Tibet.

Tibetan power spread far and wide in the later period of Trisong Detsen's reign. In the year 790, the Tibetans became very active in expansionist activities. The Tibetan army advanced westward to the Pamirs and even reached the Oxus river. As a mark of their expansion, a lake in the north of the river Oxus was named Al-Tubbat (Little Tibetan Lake). A few years later, the Arabian Caliph, Harun al-Rashid, aware that the Tibetans were becoming too powerful, allied himself with the Chinese in order to keep the Tibetans in check. Tibetans were attacked by the allied forces of the Chinese and the Arabs. However, the Tibetans were successful in holding their own without substantial loss of territory, but their expansionist dreams were checked.

King Trisong Detsen had four sons: Mutri Tsenpo, Muni Tsenpo, Mutik Tsenpo, and Tride Songtsen. The first son, Mutri Tsenpo, died young, so when Trisong Detsen retired from public life in 797, he handed over the affairs of state to his second son, Muni Tsenpo. Tibetan accounts say that Muni Tsenpo, in an effort to reduce the great disparity between the rich and the poor, introduced land reforms and appointed ministers to supervise an equitable distribution of land and property. When the king later enquired how the reform was progressing, he found to his dismay that the rich had become richer and the poor, poorer. It was found that the poor, who had become indolent during their time of ease, became poorer than ever. Yet once again, all were made to share and share alike, but without success. Disillusioned by the failure of his idealistic plan, the king is said to have consulted Padmasambhava, who informed the king that he could not forcibly close the gap between the rich and the poor. "Our condition in this life," Padmasambhava said, "is entirely dependent upon the actions of our previous life and nothing can be done to alter the scheme of things."

At least the account of the unsuccessful plans of the king shows there was an attempt to reform in the early period of Tibetan history. His rule came to an end because his mother poisoned him. After the death of Muni Tsenpo, the throne passed to the youngest son, Tride Songtsen. As he was quite young at that time, he was assisted in his rule by four experienced and capable ministers. Like his predecessors, he too carried on religious activities and expansionist policies.

Tride Songtsen had five sons: Tsangma, Darma, Ralpachen, Lhaje and Lhundup. The first born son became a monk and the last two died in childhood. When Tride Songtsen died in 815 at Drak, the ministers bypassed Darma as heir to the throne because he was irreligious, harsh, and hot tempered. They accorded royal power to Ralpachen, who was pro-Buddhist.

After ascending the throne, Ralpachen sent troops under the command of Hrangje Tsen towards the Chinese border. Buddhists in China and in Tibet sought mediation, and finally both countries sent representatives to the border. A meeting was held in AD 821 and a peace treaty concluded. The text of the treaty was inscribed on three pillars. One was erected outside the

Making of sand *mandala* (symbolising the purified area where the gods can appear) at Samye Monastery in Central Tibet. Samye is considered to be the oldest monastery in Tibet, as it was built during Padmasambhava's mission to Tibet in the eighth century.

Chinese Emperor's palace gate in Ch'angan, another on the boundary between the two countries at Gugu Meru, and the third in front of the main gate of the Jokhang at Lhasa. At the time of swearing to uphold the treaty, two religious ceremonies were performed: the Bon ritual of animal sacrifice and the Buddhist ritual of invoking the sacred trinity of the sun, moon, and stars as witnesses. With this treaty, peaceful relations were established between the two countries.

During his reign, King Ralpachen invited three Indian *pandits*, Silendrabodhi, Danasila and Jinamitra to central Tibet and provided them with two eminent translators, Kawa Paltsek and Chogro Lui Gyaltsen. The name of these translators appear at the end of almost all Tibetan books of the period, as they were responsible for the revision of the Buddhist texts, which had been translated earlier. During

their time the vocabulary used in translations was revised, and the rules of translation were laid down in detail by royal decree. A "new language" was created in this way that was more suited to translation and closer to real Tibetan than that of the first translations, which were often so literal as to be incomprehensible.

In order to build a new temple, the king sent for expert bricklayers, silversmiths and blacksmiths from China, Nepal, and Chinese Turkistan. This temple, known as Onchang Doi Lhakhang, was situated about thirty miles southwest of Lhasa near the banks of Kyichu. Ralpachen also introduced from India a new system of weights and measures for silver and grain. During his rule the priesthood was organised and enlarged, facilitating the spread of Buddhism throughout the country. To encourage people to become monks, Ralpachen decreed that seven households would have to provide for the needs of each monk. This appears to be the first case of monastic taxation in Tibet. In order to increase the respect for monks, the latter were to be known as "Priests of the King's Head." This title arose from the practice of tying to the king's hair a sheet of silk which was then spread out on the floor for the monks to sit on, while they prayed and ate before the king. This practice was followed when a monk was a guest of the king.

Not only did Indian teachers came to Tibet to teach but Tibetan monks also went to India to study Buddhism. They used to halt on the way in Nepal to learn the Indian languages. The death-toll was heavy and only a few managed to reach India. Out of a party of eight or ten, not more than two or three would return to Tibet. It is not without reason that the Tibetan fears the Indian climate.

Although King Ralpachen's reign was good for the country and its religion, some people felt that the zeal of the king was excessive. He met great opposition from his elder brother, Darma, who besides being resentful at having been denied the throne, was bitterly opposed to the Buddhist religion. So at his instigation, in the year 836 King Ralpachen was assassinated.

The pro-Bon ministers placed Darma on the throne without much opposition. Being a supporter of the Bon faith, Darma immediately set out on a violent campaign of persecution of Buddhists. Temples and monasteries were desecrated, Buddhist monks were ordered to choose either to marry, carry arms and become hunters, or else declare themselves to be followers of the Bon religion. Failure to comply with any of these orders was punishable by death. Two well known monks were executed for refusing to abandon their Buddhist faith. The Indian *pandits* and scholars, finding themselves treated with little or no respect, returned to their native land. Darma was given the name of Lang (bullock) Darma by the people because they did not like the way he treated them and their religion. There was a belief that Darma had horns on his head, and in order to hide his horns, he had arranged his hair in two plaits tied in a raised knot on each side. It is said that this is the origin of the practice of

Tibetan lay officials plaiting their hair in that manner. Within a few years Lang Darma suppressed Buddhism almost entirely in Central Tibet. By 842, religious persecution had become so intense that a monk, Lhalung Palgye Dorje, while meditating at Yerpa, decided to revolt.

Lhalung Palgye Dorje set out for Lhasa wearing a black hat and a black cloak with a white lining. He smeared charcoal on his white horse and concealed his bow and arrow in the long, flowing sleeves of his cloak. When he reached Lhasa, he left his horse tied near a *chorten* (stupa) on the bank of the river and walked into the city. He found Lang Darma and his courtiers reading the inscription of the treaty-pillar located in front of the Jokhang temple. Dancing a fantastic dance, which he had invented for the occasion, Lhalung Palgye Dorje gradually came closer to the royal presence. Lang Darma called him closer to show the dance. While making the threefold prostration which the occasion demanded, the monk drew a bow and arrow from his broad-sleeved robe and shot the king. Then he rushed to the *chorten* near the river where he had left his steed, mounted it and galloped off towards the river where he washed the charcoal from his horse, turned his robe inside out, and thus transformed, escaped to safety. This dance, now known as "The Black Hat Dance," is still celebrated throughout Tibet in commemoration of the occasion.

With Lang Darma the long line of Tibetan kings comes to an end. The unified Tibet kingdom broke up into a number of small principalities and fiefs ruled over by diverse members of the former aristocracy. These principalities were nearly always at loggerheads with each other. In this state of disorder and weakness, the Tibetans had to retreat from the land's Central Asian and south Himalayan territories.

Buddhist Renaissance

It seems ironic that the Buddhist renaissance in Tibet took place during what Tibetan historians call Sil-bu-dus, a veritable dark age that began with the fall of the monarchy system in the

Gelugpa monks debating on Buddhist philosophy and logic at Sera Monastery near Lhasa. Sera was one of the three largest monasteries in Tibet.

830s and ended with the rise of lama-rulers—the Sakya and the Dalai Lamas. This period witnessed not only a renewal but a renaissance of the four major sects of Tibetan Buddhism; most of the excellent translations of the Buddhist classics that fuelled the renaissance were also done during this period. Thus Buddhism was transformed from a religion of court into a social force which eventually engulfed the whole of Tibet. Rival royal families patronised various religious sects in a bid to regain their power and prestige. Once again the political struggle drew its vigour from rivalries between religious sects. The religious sects, having acquired great authority, became a new power in the politics of Tibet, gradually replacing noble families in terms of influence and prestige in society.

When the Mongols were carrying out their expansionist policy in the thirteenth century Tibet was also invaded by the Mongol king Changis Khan's second son, Godan Khan. In 1247, Godan Khan selected the most eminent Sakya lama of the day, Sakya Pandita, as the virtual ruler of Tibet. Godan Khan's choice of Sakya Pandita was deliberate as the Sakya lama enjoyed a high reputation in Tibet. Subsequently, the hereditary high priest of the Sakya sect was recognised by the Mongol Yuan emperors of China as the highest authority of Tibet. Thus began the system of rulers in whose hands earthly authority and the prestige of religious sanctity were united.

The ideas underlying the legitimacy of the Sakya lama's rule was a complex amalgam of Bon and Buddhist myths as well as Chinese imperial notions. At the Buddhist level, the Sakya lama claimed to be the manifestation of Manjushri, the *bodhisattva* (or he will come to this earth to relieve human suffering) of

The monastic town of Sakya which used to be the seat of the Sakyapa sect.

knowledge and wisdom. This claim probably originated with Sakya Pandita's reputation for learning. Successive Sakya lamas ruled over Tibet for about a hundred years, constituting the historic transition from royal authority based on force to lamaist authority based on religious belief.

Later, when a Mongol warrior became the Emperor of China and established the Yuan Dynasty, the emperors continued the relationship with the Sakya rulers of Tibet. This relationship formed the basis for the future unique relationship not only between the Yuan emperors and Sakya rulers but also, in recent history, between the Manchu emperors and the Dalai Lamas. The emperors of the Yuan Dynasty regarded the Sakya rulers as the highest spiritual authority. They acted as patrons to protect the lamas, their religion and people. In return, Sakya lamas provided the legitimacy required by the "barbarian" Mongol conquerors to rule over

China and their world empire. This unique interdependent relationship between the Mongol emperors of China and the Tibetan lamas came to be known as the patron-priest relationship.

In 1358, the rule of the Sakya lamas was overthrown by Changchub Galtsen, who brought nearly the whole of Tibet under his sway. He deliberately fostered a feeling of national unity and revived the traditions and glories of the earlier kings of Tibet. He inaugurated the Second Monarchy of Tibet and thus began the Phamo Drukpa period which lasted till 1434. During Changchub Galtsen's rule, the country was so secure that it was said that an old woman carrying a sackful of gold could pass without fear from one end of Tibet to the other. This period of internal security thus came to be known as the era of Genmo Serkhor ("Old Woman Carrying Gold"). The Phamo Drukpa's family was closely connected with the Sakya sect's rival, the Kagyupa sect. Phamo Drukpa's

Pelkor Choide (the golden *chorten*) in Gyantse, Central Tibet.

rule was eventually ousted in 1434 by the Rinpung princes who had the backing of the Karmapa sect. The influence of the Karmapa hierarchies was also important to the success of the Tsang kings who ruled Tibet after the Rinpung family.

These historical developments bear testimony to the fact that it was impossible for any non-priest, no matter how powerful he might have been, to rule Tibet without some religious sanction and active support provided by one religious sect or the other.

The Gelugpa sect is the last major religious sect formed in Tibetan Buddhism. Tsongkapa (1357-1419), the founder of the Gelugpa sect, aimed to reform Buddhism in Tibet by stressing on the need to return to greater austerity and spirituality. This new sect gained popularity not only within the country but also began to command the spiritual allegiance of almost all the rival tribes of Mongolia within a short span

of time. The success of the new monastic order created hostility. The Gelugpa sect, harassed by the king of Tsang, turned to the Mongols for help. In 1642, a Mongol prince, Gushi Khan, proceeded into Tibet where he defeated the king of Tsang and conferred on the head of the Gelugpa sect the title of the fifth Dalai Lama and made him the supreme authority over Tibet. Since then, ten successive Dalai Lama's have ruled over Tibet.

Institution of Dalai Lamas

In order to trace the origin of the Dalai Lamas and their ascendance to power, it is necessary to go back to the fifteenth century. The lama, who became known posthumously as the **First**

Following pages 52-53: The circumambulatory ring or Barkor in front of Jokhang Temple inevitably turns into the popular daily market.

51

Dalai Lama, was called Gendun Truppa (1391-1424). In 1415, he met Tsongkapa, the founder of the Gelugpa sect, and became one of his most important disciples.

Gedun Gyatso, born at Tanag Segme in Tsang in 1475, was considered the incarnation of Gendun Truppa and became known posthumously as the **Second Dalai Lama**. He took his first vows in 1486 and studied at Tashilhunpo and Drepung monasteries. Gedun Gyatso died in 1542 at the age of sixty-seven, at the Drepung monastery.

The following year, Sonam Gyatso was born at Tohlung near Lhasa. He was recognised as an incarnation of Gedun Gyatso, the late abbot of Drepung. Sonam Gyatso studied at Drepung monastery and took his final vows from Sonam Drakpa. He proved to be a brilliant scholar and teacher and in due course of time became the abbot of Drepung monastery.

Altan Khan of the Tumat Mongols invited Sonam Gyatso to visit Mongolia, but the lama declined. A few years later, Altan Khan sent a large delegation with camels, horses, and provisions to Tibet, again asking Sonam Gyatso to visit him. This time the lama agreed.

In the summer of 1578, the party finally arrived at a Mongolian settlement at the outpost of Chahar. A reception party sent by Altan Khan met Soman Gyatso at Chahar, and after a few more days of travel, he was welcomed by Altan Khan himself, along with a thousand cavalrymen. Together they journeyed on to the Mongol capital.

Sonam Gyatso began a programme of religious instruction for the Khan and his people and on one occasion preached in the open to the entire population. Altan Khan was converted to Buddhism. In return for his teachings, Soman Gyatso received a number of presents, together with the title, "Dalai Lama." The word "dalai" is Mongolian for "ocean" and connotes that the lama's learning was as deep and as broad as an ocean. He was also given a seal inscribed with the title "Dorje Chang" (Holder of the Thunderbolt). Sonam Gyatso then gave Altan Khan the title "Religious King, Brahma of the Gods," and prophesied that within eighty years the descendants of the Khan would become the rulers of all Mongolia and China. The title "Dalai" was retrospectively bestowed upon Sonam Gyatso's two predecessors, Gedun Truppa and Gedun Gyatso. Thus Sonam Gyatso became the **Third Dalai Lama**. It seems that Altan Khan was sincerely impressed by the spiritual teachings of the Dalai Lama and encouraged the conversion of the Mongols to Buddhism. The relationship between the Dalai Lama and the Mongol ruler was further strengthened when the great-grandson of Altan Khan was recognised as the **Fourth Dalai Lama**. He was named Yonten Gyatso.

The rulers of Tibet at that time, the Tsang king and his allies, the Karmapa, were understandably alarmed by the popularity of the Gelugpa sect. The king attacked the Drepung and Sera monasteries. The fourth Dalai Lama, Yonten Gyatso, fled from Central Tibet and later died under suspicious circumstances in 1616 at the age of twenty-five. The following year, a successor was found in the figure of Ngawang Lobsang Gyatso, born to a Nyingmapa family in the Chongyas valley. The Mongolians continued to support the Gelugpa sect. At the opportune moment, Gushi Khan defeated the king of Tsang in 1642 and Lobsang Gyatso, the **Fifth Dalai Lama**, was enthroned as regent of Tibet.

Secular and Religious Unification

The newly empowered fifth Dalai Lama set out to unite the country under Gelugpa rule. He travelled widely, inspecting the state of the monasteries and administration of the different provinces, making changes where he saw fit. By 1656, the year of Gushi Khan's death, most of Tibet was under his control. Since Gushi's successors showed little interest in Tibet, Mongolian influence waned and the Dalai Lama became virtually an absolute ruler. This was the first time in the history of Tibet that a single, indigenous regime, uniting spiritual with secular authority, truly dominated the land. The fifth Dalai Lama was generally recognised as a wise and tolerant ruler who brought back a sense of national unity and strength to Tibet.

The Dalai Lama decided to build a palace in his newly designated capital city of Lhasa.

Jowo statue in Jokhang Temple, Lhasa, is believed to be the most sacred statue in
Tibetan Buddhism.

On a hill stood the ruins of the palace, built in AD 636 by Songtsen Gampo for his Nepalese queen. The Dalai Lama selected the site for the location of his palace. The foundations were laid and the work begun in 1645. This palace was named after Mount Potala, the abode of Avalokitesvara, the Bodhisattva of compassion and is known today as the Potala Palace in Lhasa.

The fifth Dalai Lama is believed to have been the reincarnation of Avalokitesvara, who is regarded in Tibetan tradition as the founder and protector of the Tibetan race. Although the Gelugpa sect was not the first one to introduce the theory of reincarnation in Tibetan Buddhism, it proved to be of decisive importance for the Tibetan polity as it legitimised the political succession from the seventeenth century onwards. For over three hundred years, successive Dalai Lamas have been the spiritual and temporal rulers of Tibet. The Dalai Lama is

recognised as such, as he is believed to have converted the religio-political fabric of Tibet from a land torn by political and religious strife into a single nation united under a central theocratic government.

Previously, there had been constant struggles for power between different religious sects, ruling families, and powerful chiefs. The fifth Dalai Lama succeeded in winning the allegiance of the chieftains within Tibet as well as of those on the border. Taxation was just and no exemptions were made. Although he was sympathetic in dealing with his subjects, he could be ruthless in stamping out rebellion. Through his religious authority, he made his influence felt in the political affairs

Following pages 56-57: The Potala, the Dalai Lama's palace in Lhasa. The construction of Potala began in 1645 on the hillock which was the site of a palace built in AD 636 by King Songtsen Gampo.

of Mongolia and other neighbouring countries, and even among the Buddhist and Tibetan-speaking peoples of China. Although a Gelugpa himself, he retained the services of several prominent lamas from other sects. He preferred to be familiar with the beliefs and teachings of the rival sects than to remain ignorant of them. He was said to have been a good Sanskrit scholar, and he wrote many books. He established two academies, one for monk officials and one for lay officials. It is thus understandable why the Tibetan people still refer to him as the Great Fifth.

The fifth Dalai Lama did not himself exercise secular power for many years, but retired to the higher sphere of religious activities, leaving mundane affairs in the hands of his prime minister, Desi Sangye Gyatso, a man of remarkable talents. The Great Prayer festival was established on the lines on which it is celebrated today. This, the largest and most striking festival of the year in Lhasa, lasts for twenty-one days during February and March, trebling or quadrupling the population of the capital in this period.

On the twenty-fifth day of the second month of the Water-Dog Year (1682), the fifth Dalai Lama died in the Potala at the age of sixty-eight. Tibetan sources claim that his death was concealed by Sangye Gyatso for a period of fifteen years. Only the Dalai Lama's personal attendants, a monk of the Namgyal Monastery, and Desi Sangye Gyatso knew of the Dalai Lama's death. Officials and subjects alike accepted without question the Desi's announcement that the Dalai Lama had gone into meditation for an indefinite period and could not be disturbed. Anyone wishing to see the Dalai Lama on a matter of extreme urgency could only do so alone and in the privacy of the Dalai Lama's room. Meals were taken into the room as usual and everything was done to make it appear that he was alive and well. Sangye Gyatso was then carrying out a multitude of duties, including those of the Dalai Lama. In 1695, the Potala Palace was completed. In the following year, Desi Sangye Gyatso announced that the fifth Dalai Lama had died

in 1682 and that his reincarnation was already thirteen years old.

In 1697, Tsangyang Gyatso, the **Sixth Dalai Lama**, was enthroned in the Potala. He was a handsome and intelligent youth, who took his religious and political training from the Desi himself. Moreover, the Panchen Lama (the Panchen Lama is the second highest lama in the Gelugpa sect and second only to the Dalai Lama), Lozang Yeshe, visited him several times and gave him religious instructions. However, the sixth Dalai Lama turned out to be unorthodox. Instead of devoting himself to religious matters, he led a life of pleasure, beautifying his palace and grounds, resorting to drinking and the company of women. Both Desi and the Panchen Lama urged the young Dalai Lama not to lead a frivolous life nor waste his precious hours, which should be devoted to religious study. Their pleas were of no avail. The Dalai Lama began to wander off on his own, often spending his nights in Lhasa and in Shol, a small village in front of the Potala. Night after night, he roamed through the streets of Lhasa, singing drunken songs. He composed excellent, romantic verses and songs, which became very popular. Tibetans explain this behaviour as the enlightened, unfettered activity of an advanced Tantric *yogin* (practitioner). However, many Tibetans and Mongols, viewing the mode of life followed by the sixth Dalai Lama, doubted whether he could be a true incarnation of the fifth Dalai Lama.

Using the behaviour of the sixth Dalai Lama as an excuse, Lhapsang Khan, the king of Qosot (a Mongol tribe) attacked Lhasa with the consent of the Emperor of China in 1706. Desi Sangye Gyatso was killed. The Dalai Lama was declared deposed and escorted into exile. Lhapsang Khan and the Manchu emperor wanted to bring him to China, but he died in eastern Tibet before reaching the border. The people resented this treatment of the Dalai Lama and showed their displeasure by closing their shops and houses. But they could do nothing else because of the presence of Mongol troops. The Dalai Lama had managed to send a note from exile to one of his lady friends in Lhasa, in which he had written:

A chapel in Potala depicting Rig-sum-gonpo the three protecting deities of Tibet, symbolised by the three races of Bodhisattvas—Cheresi, Avalokitesvara Manjushri, and Vajrapani.

Lend me your wings, white crane;
    I go no further than Lithang,
        And thence, return again.

No one had any idea what this implied at that time; but later on, when the reincarnation of the Dalai Lama was discovered at Lithang, this message was considered prophetic.

Once the sixth Dalai Lama had been deposed, Lhapsang Khan made an announcement declaring that Tsangyang Gyatso had not been the true reincarnation of the previous Dalai Lama. He then put forth a young monk, Ngawang Yeshe Gyatso, as the true reincarnation and enthroned him in the Potala as the real sixth Dalai Lama. Ngawang Yeshe Gyatso was not generally accepted as the true reincarnation of the Dalai Lama by the people. Reports reached Lhasa that the deceased Tsangyang had been reincarnated at Lithang, and the Tibetans recalled with joy the verse quoted above. These words were held to be prophetic of his death and reincarnation.

Lhapsang Khan's position was soon under threat from another group of Mongols, the Dzungars, who were former allies of Desi Sangye Gyatso. In 1717 they invaded Tibet and murdered Lhapsang Khan. As soon as the Dzungars gained control of Lhasa, they appointed Lhagyal Rapten to be the figurehead of the Tibetan government. Ngawang Yeshe Gyatso, the so-called sixth Dalai Lama, was deposed and confined at Chakpori, a medical college established by the late Sangye Gyatso.

The Dzungars had wanted to bring Kelsang Gyatso, the **Seventh Dalai Lama,** to Lhasa and enthrone him in the Potala; but the young lama was under Manchu protection at the Kumbum monastery in Kokonor. In 1718 the Tibetans petitioned the Dzungars to bring the true Dalai Lama to Lhasa. Tsering Dondup, the Dzungar commander, promised to do so; but he could not prevail upon the Manchus to release the Dalai Lama.

Desi Lhagyal Rapten and three Tibetan officials met in secret to write a letter, saying that they recognised the young lama at Kumbum as the reincarnation of the sixth Dalai Lama, and it was sent to Kumbum. The Chinese emperor found that nearly all the Mongol tribes were in favour of the Tibetan choice. So he sent a delegation to Kumbum to offer his confirmation that Kelsang Gyatso was the reincarnation of the Dalai Lama. In 1720 the seventh Dalai Lama was enthroned.

The seventh Dalai Lama was a religious man who played a minor role in governing the country. It was left to the lay administrators, the most effective being that of Polha Sonam Topgye, who ruled until 1747. The **Eighth Dalai Lama**, Jampe Gyatso, was also largely uninvolved in matters of state, but from the time of his rule, the administration was put in the hands of a council of four ministers, one of whom would be a monk. None of the next four Dalai Lamas, from the ninth to the twelfth, had any influence over Tibetan affairs, since they all died before reaching the age of majority.

At the dawn of modern time, Tibet got mixed up in the Great Power politics. While her patron and protector, imperial China, was crumbling under the blows of the European powers and Japan, British India in the south and Russia in the north gradually maneuvered themselves into positions of strength—the former with more success than the latter. During the nineteenth century, Tibet adopted an isolationist policy and closed its borders to all foreigners.

The **Thirteenth Dalai Lama** of Tibet was Thupten Gyatso, the "Great Thirteen." In 1879, he was enthroned in the Potala. He presided over Tibet's entry into the twentieth century. He was a perceptive ruler who recognised the precious position of Tibet and the need to reach an agreement with its neighbours, especially China and British India, over the exact political status of Tibet. He was forced into exile twice during his reign: first, to Mongolia when the British, suspicious that the Tibetans were dealing with the Russians and

eager to establish their own trade agreement with Tibet, sent an expedition under Colonel Younghusband into Tibet in 1904; second, to India when the Manchus invaded in 1910 in an attempt to convert Tibet into a province of China. It marked a turning point in relations between the two countries. The patron invaded the country of his priest. Thus, the patron-priest relationship that had existed between the two countries came to an end. The fall of the Manchu Dynasty in China in 1911 removed the whole substance of personal and religious connections between the rulers of China and the Dalai Lama. The Dalai Lama returned in triumph to his capital in 1913 and issued the declaration of independence.

Later the same year, the British arranged a conference in Simla (India) between themselves, the Tibetans and the Chinese in order to establish the exact nature of the relationship between the three. The Chinese insisted that Tibet was an "integral part of China," the first time such a claim had ever been made. The Tibetans fiercely repudiated this suggestion and it was up to the British to work out some kind of compromise. The convention carried on for six months, at the end of which a series of points were drafted for official approval by the three parties concerned. The rather complex agreement hinged on the notion that Tibet was an autonomous state under the suzerainty of China. The British and Tibetans were willing to sign the agreement but the Chinese government refused. A separate Anglo-Tibetan declaration was made instead in which the British recognised Tibetan autonomy but would not recognise Chinese suzerainty over Tibet unless the Chinese signed the Simla Accord, which they never did.

For the remaining period of his rule, the thirteenth Dalai Lama had to contend with continual tension and fighting on the Chinese border as well as internal resistance to change and modernisation from the powerful and conservative elements within society. No aliens were admitted because of the fear of modernisation and even the young Tibetans who came back from England with technical knowledge were prevented from doing anything.

Altar in the interior of the Dalai Lama's private chamber in Potala.

Shortly before his death in 1933, the Dalai Lama issued a stern warning to his people of the dangers they faced ahead. But no sooner had he died than chaos and factionalism beset the government, producing the instability that Tibet could least afford at this critical time.

In 1935 Tenzin Gyatso, the **Fourteenth Dalai Lama**, was found in a humble family in the northeast of Tibet. He grew up in the seclusion of the Potala and Norbulingka palaces. Slowly and painfully he became aware of the crisis towards which his country was heading.

Diaspora

As soon as the communists came to power in China in 1949, they set about controlling Tibet effectively. Tibet found itself no match to withstand the military strength of China and there was little prospect of obtaining effective help from outside. The only viable option for Tibet was to negotiate and adjust to the new situation. A cycle of repression and resistance continued which finally culminated in the unsuccessful uprising against China in 1959. The Dalai Lama and his entourage had to escape into exile. In the following decades, more than 100,000 Tibetans followed their leader into exile. In India, Tibetans have organised themselves and got together in an effort to maintain their traditions in religion, language, literature, art, crafts, medicine and other branches of knowledge. It is in India and Nepal that Tibetan civilisation and culture are kept alive by the Dalai Lama's establishment and the Tibetan exile communities.

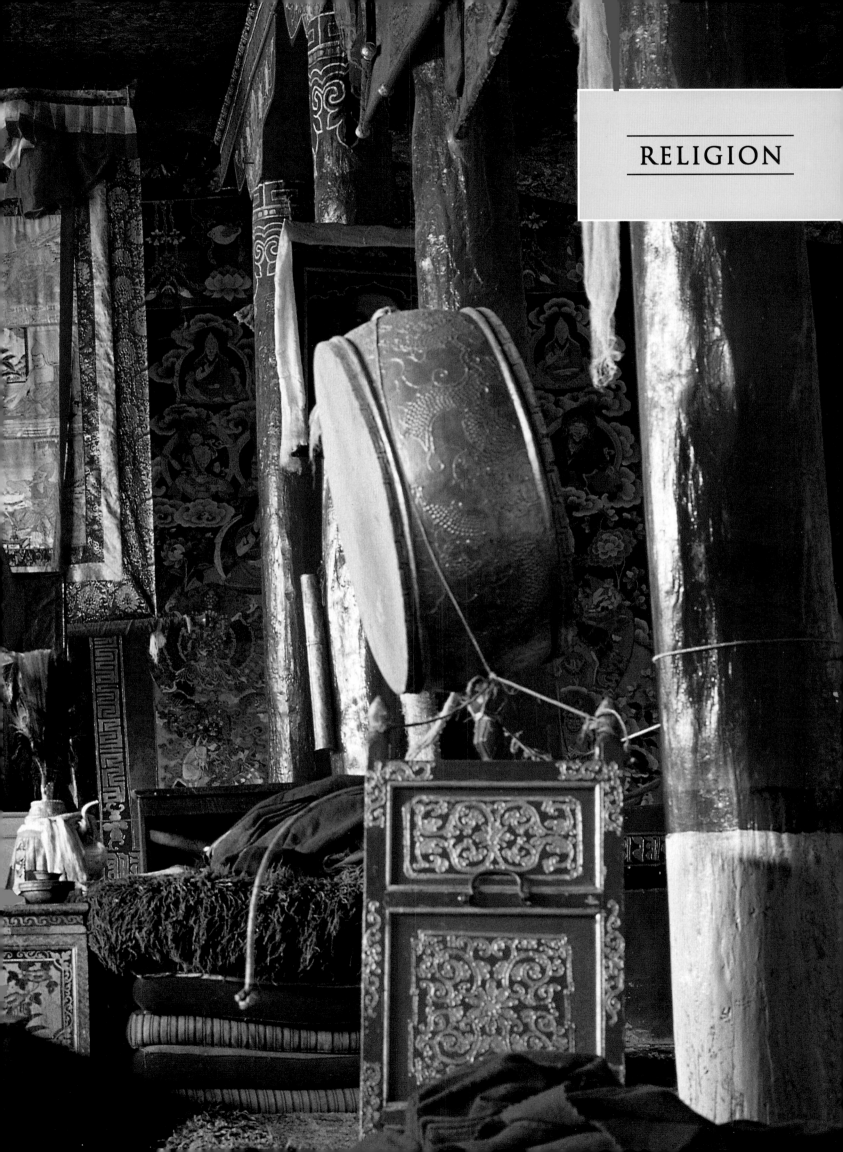

RELIGION

efore Buddhism arrived from India, the Bon religion was widespread in Tibet. It had originated in the neighbouring country, Shang Shung. Shang Shung actually existed as a non-Tibetan country at the time of the emergence of Tibet as a great power in Central Asia. It is situated to the west of Tibet. Later on, this country was annexed to Tibet. Ton-pa Shen-rab was the founder of the Bon religion and occupied a position very similar to that of the Buddha in the minds of the people. It was believed that before the appearance of Shen-rab, there existed in Tibet all sorts of demons harmful to the people. It was he, as legend goes, who made these harmful beings subservient to human requirements. He was reported to have visited many places and he had many disciples.

Bonpo

The Bon religion appears to have been a form of nature worship. Nature works on an awe-inspiring scale among the massive mountain ranges and the wide plateau of Tibet. Bon believers (Bonpos) maintained that spirits were everywhere: some good but many evil spirits dwelt in trees, under rocks, in rivers and lakes, in the sky, in mid-air and under the earth. They were probably conceived not only as inherently good or bad but also as having the power to help or to harm, to create or to destroy. The helpful ones were worshipped, and the harmful ones propitiated. The main offerings of worship or propitiatory rites were in the form of food, drink, clothing, and even stones. At first people made simple offerings themselves, but in due course the rites as well as the offerings and the recitations became increasingly complicated. Gradually, there arose a professional class of Bonpo priests. The offerings assumed various forms, including animal sacrifice, depending on the crisis to be warded off. This kind of religious life regulated all relationships between the people and the immense uncertain world of spirits.

Preceding pages 62-63: Assembly hall of Reting Monastery near Lhasa.

The development of Bon from a tribal cult in ancient Tibet into its present highly evolved form with its own body of literature, doctrines, monasteries, monks, teachings, and rules of discipline took place in stages. During the first stage, a goblin was believed to have kidnapped a boy of thirteen belonging to a Shen (priestly class) family, taken him to different places and mountains of Tibet, especially the Kham area. The boy wandered for thirteen years and was fully instructed in the demonic arts. At the age of twenty-six he was eventually allowed to return to his native place. Thanks to his training and his travels, he knew the haunts of all the malicious spirits, goblins, and demons. He could tell which of the spirits committed mischief and which of them brought good luck, as also the ways of appeasing them. Thus this young man first introduced Bon in Tibet. The earlier Tibetan kings followed Bon religion.

Not all Bonpos were native Tibetans. On the contrary, some of the Bonpo priests were invited from neighbouring countries. It was stated that at the death of king Grigum Tsanpo, the first king to leave his body on earth (his predecessors had ascended bodily to heaven by means of a rope), no one in Tibet knew how to perform the burial, and Bonpos from Ta-zig (Iran) and A-za (Afghanistan) were invited to perform the proper rituals. Thus non-Tibetan Bonpo priests were invited to Tibet because of their reputation as ritualistic experts. While the ancient Bonpo priests may have had a number of varied functions, their chief function seems to have been connected with the funeral ceremonies of the kings and the subsequent cult which took place on the burial mound. They enjoyed royal patronage. Later on, Bon underwent changes due to the influence of the heretical Shaivite (Lord Shiva theism) doctrine.

Bon religion prevailed in Tibet without a rival till Buddhism came, first in the sixth century AD and more strongly in the seventh and eighth centuries. The introduction of Buddhism under royal patronage during the seventh and eighth centuries naturally provoked the opposition of the native religion. The Bonpo priests were supported by powerful aristocratic families violently opposed to those Buddhist groups who enjoyed the particular favour of the royal house and who designated their doctrine as *chos (dharma* or the sacred duty*)*. In due course, the religious struggles of the eighth and ninth centuries led to the collapse of the Tibetan state in 842 and the disintegration of the royal dynasty. The Bonpo priesthood, along with its doctrines and practices utterly vanished as an organised, religious body. Certainly many elements of their religion must have survived but there is a definite dissolution of continuity in the religious history of Tibet during the dark and confused period following the collapse of the dynasty.

When an organised Bonpo tradition re-emerges in the eleventh century, it is nothing less than an entirely different religion. It is essentially a lamaist school. It is true that the divinities of the Bonpo pantheon have other names and also differ in iconographic detail from those of other Tibetan Buddhist schools. It is also true that there are superficial differences in symbolism and ritual behaviour between Bonpos and Tibetan Buddhists: thus the Bonpos circumambulate holy places and holy objects, always keeping them to their left, and not, as other Tibetans, to their right; likewise they turn their prayer-wheels, and the like, in a sinistral instead of a dextral fashion, and instead of the famous *mantra* (ritual chant), *"Om mani padme hum"* ("We follow in path of the Jewel," that is, the Buddha), they recite a different *mantra*, *"Om matri mu ye sale'du"* which has the same significance.

Bonpo monks, like monks of the other Tibetan Buddhist schools, strive to attain Buddhahood, following the same path of scholastic study, ritual practice, and meditational experience; they have the same concept of the world as an opposition between the state of suffering and impermanence, of ignorance and limitation on the one hand, and of spiritual existence, infinite insight, and non-spatial, non-temporal transcendence on the other. At least since the fifteenth century they have a tradition of monastic life, on the same lines as that of the Tibetan Buddhist schools.

Bonpo monasteries existed all over Tibet. Even in Central Tibet, the very centre of Gelugpa orthodoxy, the Bonpos had monasteries with several hundred monks. They have re-established centres, even in exile, where the followers of Bon pursue deep study and meditation.

Buddhism

Buddhism entered Tibet from India in two principal phases. The first phase was during the reign of the Yarlung kings. It was king Lha-tho-tho-ri Nyantsen of Tibet who first introduced Buddhism to Tibet well over a thousand years ago. It spread steadily, and in the course of time many renowned *pandits* (religious teachers) of India came to Tibet and translated Buddhist texts of the *Sutras* (discourses of the Buddha) and the *Tantras* with their commentaries. The Indian *pandit* who is most associated with this period is Padmasambhava. Religious activities suffered a setback for some years during the reign of King Lang Darma in the tenth century; but that temporary eclipse was soon dispelled, and Buddhism revived and spread again, starting from the eastern and western parts of Tibet. This second phase was started in the eleventh century, Atisha and Milarepa being the best known figures of this time.

The teachings of the Buddha which have been translated into Tibetan are contained in over one hundred volumes, known collectively as the *Kangyur*. Although such a large number of volumes has been compiled, the actual extent of the teachings of the Buddha cannot, in fact, be measured. Moreover, there are also a great many commentaries to these teachings of the Buddha. In addition, numerous other works written by many eminent *gurus* (teachers) and erudite *pandits* of India include commentaries on all four classes of the secret Tantra teachings, advanced meditation, and oral tradition teachings. Because of the great kindness of the ancient translators and *pandits*, more than two hundred volumes of such commentaries have been translated into Tibetan and collectively they are known as the *Tangyur*. It is these texts, then, which formed the foundation for Buddhism in Tibet.

A part of the Monlam festival (Great Prayer Festival) in Lhasa.

Buddhist Sects

In the course of time different schools of Tibetan Buddhism, originating from a single source, have emerged due to the special stress each has laid on particular aspects of liturgy and doctrine. A very crude way of distinguishing the two principle schools in Tibet is by the colour of the hats the members wear on ceremonial occasions. "Red" denotes all the non-reformed schools from the Nyingmapas to the Kagyupas, whilst "yellow" refers to the reformed school founded by Tsongkhapa. The Tibetans sometimes distinguish between what they call the Old Ones and the New Ones, the former being the Nyingma order, which bases its teachings on the first translations that were done from the seventh century onwards, and the latter being the Sakya, Kagyu and Gelug orders, who base their traditions upon the later translations begun in the eleventh century. This is a much more helpful distinction than simply that of distinguishing the sects as the Red and Yellow Hats.

Another way of dividing the sects is through historical division: the Nyingmapa are the earliest order; the Sakya and Kagyu are the middle orders; and the Gelug the later order. Apart from these four major sects, each of these sects have further sub-sects. However, all Tibetans describe themselves as *Nangpa* (all inside the Law, that of the Buddha), and seldom do they describe themselves by their sects. All the four sects adhere to all the teachings of the major Buddhist schools, the Hinayana, Mahayana and Tantrayana, for Tibetan Buddhists do not separate these teachings, but pay equal respect to them all. For moral guidance, they conform to the Vinaya rules which are principally followed by Hinayanists, while for more esoteric practices, of every degree of profundity, they use the

Young unreformed lamas performing their rituals in a street corner, Lhasa.

methods of the Mahayana and Tantrayana rules.

Nyingmapa

The only sect of Tibetan Buddhism which could lay claim to an origin earlier than the second spread of the doctrine is the Nyingmapa, the followers of the old school. This sect is usually considered to be founded by Padmasambhava because a large bulk of the Nyingmapa scriptures are connected with him. Padmasambhava came from Uddiyana or Swat, a famous centre of religious syncretism in the northwestern region of India. He is popularly known as Guru Rimpoche, the "Precious Teacher." Guru Rimpoche was an extremely able and astute Buddhist Tantric master. By his spells and incantations, Guru Rimpoche is reputed to have overcome the malignant demons who prevented the progress of

Buddhism. Having conquered them, he is said to have enlisted their aid for the protection of Buddhism. Realising the hold the Bon faith still had over many of the people, Guru Rimpoche incorporated many Bon beliefs, practices, and deities into the Buddhist ritual. Ritualistic cannibalism and human sacrifice he discontinued, but black magic and the old Bon oracles he retained. He then founded the first large monastery to be built in Tibet. He chose Samye, thirty miles southeast of Lhasa, for the site and fashioned the construction after the model of Odantapuri in northern India. Samye monastery is one of the most important monasteries in Tibet.

The main doctrines of the Nyingmapa are sub-divided into nine vehicles. When these nine are grouped together, they can be classified into two categories: Causal Vehicles and Resultant Vehicles. In brief, the Causal Vehicles are stages of practice for collecting merit and insight, while

67

the Resultant Vehicles are stages of practice during which one has the complete authority to visualise oneself, while still unenlightened, as having the forms and bodies that will be attained once enlightenment is achieved. The teachings concerning the "Intermediate State" or "Bar-do" are common to all schools of Tibetan Buddhism. Only the Nyingmapa version of the "Bar-do" has been studied and translated. "Bar-do thodrol" means "salvation by the mere hearing (of the holy text) when in the Intermediate State." The text is whispered into the ear of the dying person or a dead man. It is also studied during one's lifetime so that the individual may find his way through the deceptions and terrors of his earthly state.

The Nyingmapa tradition is also known as the Terma, "Treasure Text Tradition." This is because the great teacher Guru Rimpoche buried his teachings in the earth for the sake of the protection and preservation of the *dharma* (i.e. Buddhism, or *buddhadharma*) against future degenerate times. There were actually two types of Treasure Texts: *Sayi Ter,* or the Ground Treasure Texts of teachings buried by Guru Rimpoche himself, and *Gongpai Ter,* or the Allied Treasure Texts of teachings buried by the lamas who followed after Guru Rimpoche and who received these teachings in dreams and in clear visions. Later, when the times were right, subsequent lamas and incarnations of Guru Rimpoche unearthed these Treasure Texts.

Kagyupa

The eleventh century was a period of great innovation in Tibetan religion, and it marked the beginning of a wide range of different lineages and traditions of teaching. Perhaps the greatest stimulus to religious developments in Tibet in the eleventh century was the mission of the great Indian teacher Atisha, who arrived in Tibet in 1042 at the age of sixty after repeated invitations from the religious kings of Western Tibet. He had studied and taught at the Indian monastic universities of Bodhgaya, Odantapuri and Vikramashila and he was probably the most famous and revered religious teacher in India at the time. He remained in Tibet until his death in 1054. Atisha, along with his disciple Brom-ton founded the Kadampa tradition from which Kagyu, Sakya and Gelug traditions subsequently emerged. It was Marpa who introduced Kagyupa sect, that is, "The Succession of Orders" in Tibet. It is based on the oral teachings of its guru or the secret, esoteric teachings passed on from teacher to disciple by word of mouth. Marpa received his initiation from Naropa, one of the most famous Vajrayana (Tantric Buddhist) teachers of the time. Marpa had already learnt Sanskrit at the age of fifteen. While still a young man he sold his possessions for gold and made his way to India. There he found his Guru, Naropa, not far from Nalanda. He was warmly received by the great Vajrayana teachers and initiated into profound doctrines. He was taught the doctrine of Mahamudra, the "Great Symbol," which means the convergence of the universe in the higher consciousness. One of the most important doctrines Marpa received from his guru was "The Six Principles of Naropa."

The main disciple of Marpa was the great ascetic and poet, Milarepa. Milarepa, after a most moving experience, was initiated by Marpa after which he avoided all contacts with society. He was frequently called "Cotton Clad Mi-la," because he lived on the Tibetan mountains, clad only in a single cotton garment; but often known simply as "The Revered Mi-la." First a wizard, then a saint, and always a poet, his songs, as well as his biography, are widely read and often quoted. Milarepa became the heir of all teachings of the Kagyupa. His teachings included what were known as the "Six Principles of Naropa." He had eight spiritual souls and thirteen lesser souls. Of the former groups, Rechung and Gampopa are the most important. Since Rechung was a Buddhist mainly interested in his own practical experience of the Vajrayana secrets, the main stream of the Kagyupa tradition did not flow through him but through Gampopa. Gampopa was already thirty-two when he met Milarepa and became his

Preceding pages 68-69: Powa (death ritual) in Drigung, Central Tibet. Powa is a consciousness transfer ritual in which the consciousness of a person who has just died is transferred to his next rebirth.

Senior lamas conducting Losar (New Year) ceremony at Jokhang Temple, Lhasa.

disciple. Milarepa transmitted all teachings to him, including the "Six Principles of Naropa."

Generally, the Kagyupa sect favours Tantric rites and the deeper practices of Yoga, convinced that the divine light hidden in man can reveal itself to the adept in its saving purity through appropriate Yoga exercises and meditations. This is the essence of the *zokchen* (the great perfection or completion) teaching.

Sakyapa

The Sakya school received its name from the colour of the soil at the site of its first monastery. In Tibetan *sa* is earth and white is called *kya*. In course of time the name Sakya prevailed. The cause and fruit or effect doctrine of this school goes back to the translator Drogme, who studied in India and was the most important teacher to the founder of the Sakya monastery. Drogme set out for India and

Nepal with the financial assistance of the local Tibetan ruler of western Tsang. Having studied Sanskrit intensively for a year in Nepal, he pursued his textual and religious studies at Vikramashila for eight years under the guidance of the Great Buddhist Tantric master, Santipa. He was initiated into a series of texts. One such text is the *Hevajra-Tantra*, on which Santipa had written an important commentary, and it was Drogme who later translated this into Tibetan with the result that it subsequently became one of the basic texts of the Sakya order. The tutelary deity of the Sakyapa is Dorje Phurpa. Another deity, Manjushri, is also of great significance and importance in this school.

The Sakya monastery was founded in 1073 by Konch'og Gyelpo (1034-1102) of the Khon

Following pages 72-73: A giant Buddha *tangkha* hanging on the walls of Drepung Monastery, inaugurating Lhamo (opera) festival in Lhasa.

71

Black hat dance performed by a lama in Kham, Eastern Tibet.

family. Gyelpo was a disciple of Drogme. It was his son and successor, the Great Kunga Nyingpo (1092-1158), who consciously formulated all the teachings received, and it is only from his time onwards that it is possible to refer to a specifically Sakya school. With local patronage and keen organising powers of Kunga Nyingpo, the wealth and fame of the Sakya sect grew rapidly. Kunga Gyaltsten, known as the Sakya Pandita, was especially significant for the development of the spiritual and secular hierarchy of the sect. Under his leadership the secular dominance of the Sakya lamas was recognised all over Tibet.

Gelugpa

Gelugpa means the "followers of the Virtuous Order." This school was founded at the beginning of the fifteenth century AD by Tsongkapa. At the time of the birth of

Tsongkapa a great deal of degeneracy and laxness had crept into monastic discipline. Due to the rivalry over temporal powers between the Sakyapa and Kagyupa, spiritual and intellectual pursuits were often neglected. Both exoteric and esoteric Buddhism was at a low tide in Tibetan cultural areas. With the exception of the best few, the majority of the priests did not observe the strict rules of monastic discipline. Those who developed intellectually did not have spiritual realisation. Those who indulged in esotericism were more interested in rituals than in their meaning. Tsongkapa first emphasized the importance of monastic discipline by insisting on proper monastic garments and other badges for the order, to distinguish it from the rest of the population. Second, he gave primary importance to the inner urge of wanting the welfare of others as the key to further development. Third, strict guidance from the masters was made mandatory for those who

74

Lama musicians playing *gyaling* (the horn-like trumpets) at the beginning of Cham (lama ritual dance) in Kham.

practised esotericism. Finally, in order to correct the tendency to make premature advances, he made a science of Buddhist philosophy by outlining the actual process from intellectual understanding to spiritual realisation. When he was fifty, he founded the Ganden monastery. He also blessed the founding of Drepung and Sera monasteries by his disciples. These are the three most famous monasteries of the Gelugpa.

The first two successors of Tsongkapa in the abbacy of Ganden were his close disciples. The third was a younger follower, Gendun Truppa (1391-1475), who is said to have been Tsongkapa's nephew. It was his energy and ability which was mainly responsible for building up Tsongkapa's school into an active expansive order ready and anxious to compete with the others on an equal footing. The most striking feature of this school is the manner in which it practised the theory of reincarnation. This school firmly believed that the protector of

Tibet, Avalokitesvara, is permanently reincarnated in a series of monks beginning with Gendun Truppa, the first Dalai Lama. As such Gendun Truppa was to become the first Dalai Lama; and the first abbot of Tashilhunpo monastery was to become the first Panchen Lama, though they were not referred to by the above names during their lifetime. In addition to these four main Tibetan traditions, there are other minor traditions from which many other additional aspects of Tantric practice are derived. But all of these many traditions, except for their having different names, do not differ much. In essence they all come together on one point: each and every one of them teaches methods for accomplishing the same ultimate goal, the full enlightenment of Buddhahood.

Following page 76: A woman spinning wool at Phuntsoling village in Central Tibet.

Top left: Lhasa woman carrying her baby in the typical Tibetan style. **Right:** Churning buttermilk, Damshung, Central Tibet.
Bottom left: Woman pilgrim from Kongpo, Southern Tibet, on the way to Lhasa. **Right:** Once a nomad, this woman has now settled in a mud house, Damshung village, Central Tibet.

The headgear worn by Tibetans often identifies the region they come from. **Top left:** Ceremonial hat from the U-Tsang. **Right:** Typical pastoral headgear from Central Tibet. **Bottom left & right:** Hats made of fox hair worn by the Khampa (those belonging to the Kham region). **Facing page:** A man from Central Tibet

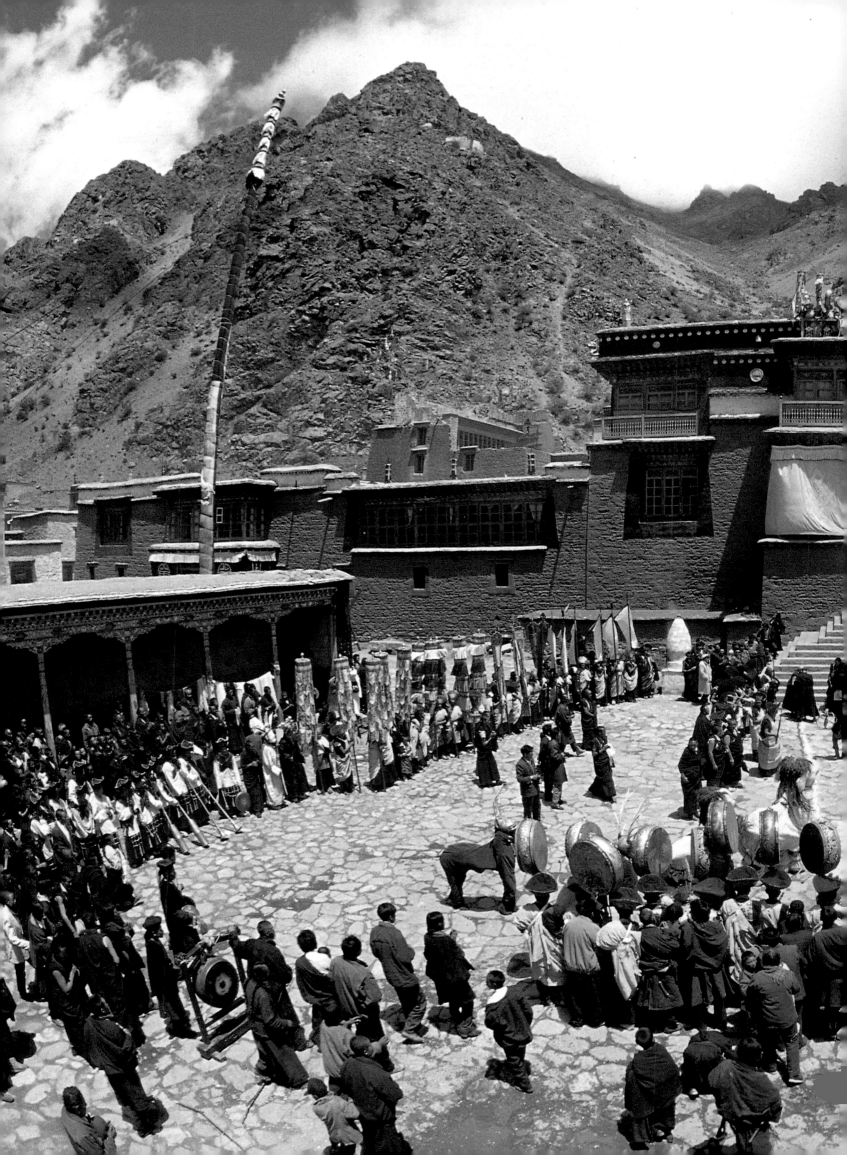

FESTIVALS...

AND
CEREMONIES

Every Tibetan festival has a special religious significance and a characteristic way of celebration. Festivals are great levellers and help people of all strata to interact and mix. For the Tibetans living in exile, these festivals are very important as they provide an opportunity to meet and conglomerate, giving them a sense of belonging.

LOSAR (New Year): The New Year (Losar), is the most popular festival. It falls in the first week of the first month of the Tibetan year, which corresponds to late February or early March. A number of preparatory ceremonies precede it which are meant to chase away evil spirits and welcome the future. All homes are cleaned. Special attention is paid to the kitchen to appease Thaplha, the hearth god.

At the celebratory feast a couple of days before the New Year, a ritual dance used to be performed by the monks of the Namgyal monastery to the heady beat of drums and sound of long trumpets (*radong*), in the courtyard of the Potala Palace, which was witnessed by the Dalai Lama himself and hundreds of people who come from far away. This ceremony is now replicated in Dharamsala. After the dance, the lead dancer comes forward and in a symbolic gesture pours spirit from a skull over a cauldron of boiling oil. Evil spirits, sketched on a piece of cloth suspended over the fire are thus destroyed and a fresh year begins.

The eating of *guthug* (a dumpling soup made of nine ingredients), is another important aspect of the celebrations. The dumplings are made of wheat flour and have various objects placed inside them, like charcoal, hot pepper, threads or pieces of paper, each indicating some trait of the human personality. Thus each diner's personality is judged by the

object he finds in his dumpling. In an elaborate follow-up ritual all members of the family pour their soup into another bowl, called the witch's bowl, with a dough figure of a witch in it. Prayers are chanted to drive away evil, illness and impurity from the house. Finally one of the family runs with the bowl and a torch to the end of the village or town.

On the first dawn of the New Year, the wife or matriarch of the family goes to collect the year's first bucket of water. She burns incense to appease the water deities. Prayers are recited, and lamps lit; with the rest of the week being spent in merrymaking.

MONLAM CHENPO (Great Prayer Festival of Lhasa): A few days after the New Year celebrations comes the Molam Chenpo or the Great Prayer Festival which was founded by Tsonghapa at Jokhang in 1409. He intended it as a kind of annual revival and rejuvenation of the Buddhist faith. This festival was held every year in Tibet until 1959. Nearly 20,000 monks used to congregate in Lhasa to pray during these celebrations, which lasted for twenty-one days. Contributions by private establishments and individuals were made in the form of money or foodstuffs.

Prior to 1959 this festival used to be conducted in Tibet under the supervision of Drepung monastery. It is celebrated on the fifteenth of the month of Losar, the day when Buddha Sakyamuni, through his miraculous abilities, defeated the six Brahmanical teachers. On this day, the Dalai Lama was present and used to be greeted by the Nechung oracle, making his way in a trance to the main Jokhang. In the absence of the Dalai Lama, the Ganden Throne Holder used to act as the presiding master of the prayer ceremony. The entire monastic population assembled for a prayer congregation. If the Dalai Lama was present, he used to hold discourses on the Buddha's previous lives. At dusk, he used to inspect the huge butter sculptures displayed by the monks and evaluate them according to their artistic merit.

On the twenty-fourth day of the first month of the year, the ceremony marking the completion of the Great Prayer Festival, called

Preceding pages 80-81: Tsorphu monastery, the traditional seat of Karmapas, head of the Kargyupa sect. **Pages 82-83:** Horse racing at Paiyual in Kham, Eastern Tibet. **Facing page:** Masked lamas perform a welcome dance during a High Lama's visit to Tsorphu monastery near Lhasa.

84

the Propitiation Ceremony of the Prayer Festival (Monlam Torgyap) is held. It is dedicated to the life of the Dalai Lama. Hundreds of men dressed as olden-day warriors firing hand-guns walk in a huge procession along with monks to the festival site. A large number of cavalry in ancient costumes and armour takes part. In symbolic terms, the site of the propitiation ceremony is the battleground of a spiritual war between the forces of good and evil.

SAGA DAWA (Buddha's Parinirvana Month):

The fourth month of the Tibetan calendar is regarded as very auspicious. Prayers are held throughout the month in various monasteries. The fifteenth day of this month is the most important day for Tibetan Buddhists, as it was the day on which Buddha Sakyamuni was conceived by his mother, Queen Mayadevi. Thirty-five years later, on the same day of the same month, Buddha was believed to have tamed a host of demons at dusk, and in the early dawn of the sixteenth day to have attained complete Enlightenment. Tradition also records that he passed into *parinirvana*, the ultimate state of peace, at Kushinagara on the same day fifty years later.

In fact, the whole month is believed to possess so much potency that the effect of anything, either good or bad, that one does is multiplied a hundred thousand times. The whole month is hence declared a meatless month, since the taking of one life would be regarded as equal to the taking of a hundred thousand lives. From the first day of the month, silences are observed, the devout start penance and many undertake fasts. Offerings and charity are redoubled on this day. People also save the lives of slaughter animals by buying them and setting them free. The most popular way to acquire merit is to circumambulate around the monasteries. Hence from the first day of the month, one finds people busy walking round the monasteries, turning prayer wheels and beads.

DZAM-LING CHI-SANG (World Purification Day):

The fifteenth day of the fifth Tibetan lunar month is celebrated as the Dzam-ling Chi-sang (World Purification Day), to commemorate the successful completion of Samye monastery. This festival began during the reign of King Trisong Deutsen (8th century AD) when holy men subdued and bound to oaths all spirits and ghosts hindering the building of Samye monastery. Some of these spirits and ghosts were summoned through oracles and consulted for predictions in order to enhance the building of the monastery. This event is also seen as the beginning of the deity invocation rite in Tibetan Buddhist culture. The spirits and deities were appeased through a grand offering of incense. King Trisong Deutsen commissioned a grand purification rite of incense burning and prayer flags to be performed on Hepo-ri hilltop in order to purify the cosmic energy and the environment.

Throughout Tibet, people burn incense as a purifying agent and prayer flags made in five different colours—blue, white, red, green and yellow, symbolising the sky, cloud, fire, water and the earth respectively—are flown. The ingredients used for burning are fragrant trees, herbs like cyprus, juniper, rhododendrons, white and red sandalwood and saffron. Raising prayer flags, burning incense and circumambulating hills have been native Tibetan customs practised before the introduction of Buddhism, and these have been incorporated into Buddhist rituals.

WANGKOR (Making the Rounds of the Field):

In the Tibetan countryside, the Wangkor is considered the important festive occasion. It is celebrated throughout the farming areas of Tibet, when the crops ripen and expresses the farmer's wishes for a bumper harvest. "Wang" means field and "kor" means a round, so the name literally implies "making rounds of the fields." This festival constitutes a delightful break for the otherwise busy farmers. The date of the festival differs from place to place. In the Lhasa region, it starts on August 1, and carries on for three to five days. In the regions of Gyantse and Shigatse,

Facing page: Lamas carrying a deity for worship.
Following pages 88-89: The heart of the Tibetan home is in the kitchen. A Tibetan lady churning salted butter tea in a *jhadong* (cylindrical tea churner).

One of the non-Tibetan sports introduced in Tibet by the Chinese is billiards. The new game is popular even among the nomads of Chanthang, Northern Tibet.

Wangkor is celebrated in mid-July. The festival goes back nearly 1,500 years when King Pude Gongyal wanted to guarantee good harvests and hence requested Bon priests for help. The priests instructed the farmers to walk around the fields in order to get Heaven's blessings for a good harvest. It began merely as a pre-harvest ritual, but gradually became a traditional festival. Entertainment on these days used to consist of contests such as wrestling and fencing, to which horse-races, archery and Tibetan opera were included with the passage of time. With the spread of Buddhism in Tibet, the practice of carrying the sacred Buddhist book (the *Bum*), and statues of Buddha in procession round the fields came to be included.

LHABAB DUCHEN (Buddha's Descent from Tushita Heaven): The day of Buddha Sakyamuni's descent from the Tushita god-realm to Sankhasa in the city of Kashi, is celebrated as Lhabab Duchen. Buddha Sakyamuni is said to have travelled at the age of forty-one to Tushita heaven, where his mother Mahamaya had taken rebirth as one of the gods. In order to repay his mother's kindness, he spent one rainy season-retreat at Tushita, giving innumerable teachings to his mother and the host of gods. Nobody knew where Buddha Sakyamuni had gone for the duration of the retreat. Soon after the conclusion of the three-month retreat, Maudgalyayanputra, who had acted as Buddha's regent in the human world, used his miraculous powers to go to the god-realm and invite the Buddha back to this world. Buddha agreed to return on the twenty-second day of the ninth month of the Tibetan year. He told Maudgalyayanputra to return to the human world to inform his disciples there.

With great excitement, the entire circle of his followers cleaned the city and prepared for Buddha's return. On the orders of Lord Indra,

Barkor Square in Lhasa. The name derives from the word barkor, the religious route (*parikrama*) along which pilgrims and devotees used to circumambulate in holy places.

Vishvakarma, the divine craftsman, miraculously erected three ladders. Buddha descended halfway to this earth by using one staircase and the other half using his miraculous powers. To commemorate this descent of Buddha, devout followers of both gods and men built *stupas* having four or eight circular steps. Tibetan Buddhists celebrate this day by devoting it to religious activities, such as visiting temples, lighting butter lamps, chanting *mantras*, reading scriptures, and trying to accumulate as many merits as possible.

GANDEN NGACHOD (The Festival of Lights): The twenty-fifth day of the tenth Tibetan month is commemorated as the death anniversary of Tsongkapa, the celebrated founder of the Gelugpa sect. It is also known as the Festival of Lights as a large number of butter-fed lamps are lit on the roofs of every household and monasteries at dusk, presenting a unique sight,

as the lamps twinkle like distant stars. It is a feast reminiscent of the Diwali festival of India, and takes place at roughly the same time (October-November).

NGANPA GUZOM (Day of Ten Auspicious Signs): The period from noon of the sixth day of the eleventh Tibetan month (December-January) until noon the following day, is regarded as extremely inauspicious. Tibetans are exhorted not to start any new ventures during this period which lasts for twenty-four hours.

These inauspicious hours are followed by the "day of ten," celebrated as the day of ten auspicious signs. This auspicious period also lasts for twenty-four hours, during which people meet each other, go on picnics and have fun.

Following pages 92-93: Cham (lama dance) at Kathok Monastery in Kham, Eastern Tibet. **Pages 94-95:** Sky burial in Drigung, Central Tibet. As a last act of charity, the dead body in Tibet is given to vultures.